FARM DON'T HUNT

THE DEFINITIVE GUIDE TO

CUSTOMER SUCCESS

GUY NIRPAZ

with Fernando Pizarro

Copyright

TABLE OF CONTENTS

ACKNOWLEDGMENTS

I'd like to thank all that have contributed to the creation of this book and to the reviewers that have provided feedback through many drafts:

Mikael Blaisdell, Omer Gotlieb, Boaz Maor, Dustin Markowski, Kaiser Mulla-Feroze, Maksim Ovsyannikov, Oren Raboy, Mark Roberge, Ophir Sweiry, Jacco Van Der Kooij and many of Totango's customers that have shared their valuable time with me.

Dedication

To - Limor, Ori, Gali and Rotem - my true inspiration.

Foreword

The disciplines of marketing and sales have traditionally owned a controlling stake in building customer relationships. On the surface, this makes a certain amount of sense: We need to make customers aware of our offerings and get them in the door.

And certainly, this focus on attracting, or hunting, new customers has been a short-term win for businesses—a fix for executives and shareholders who need the instant gratification of higher and higher revenues at the end of the each quarter.

But for many hunters, the long-term results have been disastrous. That's because these organizations have failed to understand and focus on the entirety of the customer journey. Specifically, they've neglected those touchpoints and interactions that come after the point of sale. They've ignored the needs that customers have as they actually learn, use, and get help with a product or service.

We've all seen the telltale signs of the hunting approach. Incomprehensible airline fare rules, draconian return policies, labyrinthine automated phone systems, insolent employees, and rage-inducing user interfaces have plagued the customer experience for decades.

So it shouldn't come as a surprise when fed-up customers have, in turn, spent less money with a company, taken their business elsewhere, and warned their friends to steer clear. It's what any of us would do if we were treated badly, had to jump through hoops to get the value that we'd paid for, or simply couldn't find the value in what we had purchased.

But your company and your customers don't have to go down this path. In this book, Guy elucidates the farming approach to customer relationships. Following his advice will put you on the path to long-term customer and business success.

Kerry Bodine

Co-author of: *Outside In: The Power of Putting Customers at the Center of Your Business*

Chapter 1

Introduction

This book is written for the leaders of recurring revenue and subscription businesses. In it, I offer a framework and operational guidance that will help maximize customer retention, minimize customer churn, and maximize customer lifetime value.

The lessons that follow are based on the many years I spent building a software platform for Customer Success at the company I founded, Totango, and the time I spent as a business leader prior to that. Most importantly, they reflect the sum of all the learning I have gained from the best teachers of all – my customers.

The first half of the book provides the structure for you to think about your Customer Success efforts – what I believe is the fundamental difference between the Customer Success paradigm and the traditional view of customer management. The second half of the book provides practical advice for managing customers under this new paradigm.

The Hunt for Customers

The crux of every business is the customer relationship. The customer buys something from the seller. That transaction is the heart of every company, big or small, high tech or low. And, until recently, the prevailing perception of the customer relationship was most akin to a hunt. Highly commissioned salespeople were incentivized to bring down large or numerous accounts. It's no wonder that successful salespeople were called hunters and the terms used to describe the relationship evoked the chase, the funnel, and the close. The entire company as well as the sales staff was oriented around the sale, not the ongoing relationship.

A Change in the Customer Relationship

The last ten years or so have seen the growth of several factors that have led to a fundamental change in that customer relationship, factors that have created a great deal of disruption and corresponding opportunity. This disruption has been felt across almost all functions of business and sectors of the economy, but it has exerted a particular impact on the how businesses interact with their customers and the way in which those customers must be managed.

The Rise of Recurring Revenue Businesses and Business Models

The first major change has been the rise of the recurring revenue business model in the B2B world and of subscription and partial ownership models in the broader economy. In this new model, customers pay on a monthly or annual basis for products or services that they can discontinue at any time. And rather than closing the customer once and considering them "bagged," the seller must work hard to make sure they are continually satisfied, and, more importantly, successful. The fact that the seller does not get paid up front has shifted the pattern of investment in the customer away from an all out, one-off effort to score a big payoff to a pattern of periodic investment in customer outcomes that ideally synchronizes with the payment stream from the customers.

Digitization Affects All Products and Customer Experiences

Back in 2009, I was sitting in the restaurant car on the Eurostar barreling from Paris to Amsterdam when the Green Revolution in Iran broke out. At the time I was already a fairly avid Twitter user, but it was that event unfolding in real time that really got me to thinking about how fundamentally digital our world had become. As I sat there, an Iranian client of mine was tweeting about what he was seeing, and I could literally see his data feed and others coming from a very complicated situation, informing the world of developments in near real time. And in a sort of 'aha' moment I realized that this level of digitization would revolutionize the business world as well, helping to make the hunt for customers a thing of the past.

You see, we live in a time when almost all products are acquiring a digital component. This means that there is a real time stream of information being generated by every interaction the customer has with products and services. This digitization of product use makes complete transparency—everything the customer knows about their use of the product can and should be known to the seller, so it becomes possible to monitor that use and take action to ensure it is adding value for the customer. This is clearly true if the product is something like a Customer Relationship Management (CRM) software platform, but even in the case of non-digital items like toasters ordered via Amazon, both the customer and the business know when the product was ordered, when it was delivered, what other products the customer browsed, and so on. And even in the case of a toaster, it won't be long before the act of toasting a bagel will generate a real time data feed too, which will make it possible for the toaster maker to know when the product was used, how often, and by whom, which will allow them all kinds of insight into the customer use case and its value. Moreover – to compete, the toaster maker will have to work to ensure that the toasting experience is a good one long after the initial purchase.

Increased Customer Expectations

The third change in the customer relationship is the rapid increase in customer expectations. That bar has been set in the consumer space by highly responsive firms like Google, Facebook, Amazon, and Linkedin, companies that have made their products easy to use, highly value-additive, and responsive to the aggregate demands of their user base. This development in the customer relationship is the one that left B2B firms most vulnerable, because most have not mastered an environment where paying customers are just a click away from trying out the next new thing.

Customers, in other words, are no longer prey whose yield you capture at sale. Rather, they are like plants that must be encouraged to take root and nurtured through their lifecycle, their yield gathered over time.

So, as a business, you can no longer hunt them. They must be farmed.

Chapter 2

Customer Success – The Farming Paradigm

If, in this new world, your customers must be farmed not hunted, then Customer Success is the farming paradigm. As a concept, Customer Success has been around for just a few years. In fact many business leaders are still unclear on what exactly Customer Success entails. That's why the farming metaphor is useful.

Think of a farmer. While not particularly sophisticated, he maximizes his harvest with simple tasks that he repeats every year. He prepares the soil. He carefully tends to young seedlings. He provides his crop with attention, water, and fertilizer over time to ensure that his harvest will be healthy not only this year, but in years to come. He identifies problems and tests solutions, keeping only what works.

If you think of farming your customers rather than hunting them, then what you know about farming takes on new meaning. Simple repetitive farming tasks become replicable business processes. Tending to new plants becomes onboarding your customers on your product. And all of the things you provide your plants have business equivalents in terms of time, money, and attention. Crucially, when farming, the goal is to profit over many years; any single plant will have many harvests. This concept of nurturing and a long-term horizon is the opposite of hunting with its upfront reward and short-term focus. While there are some exceptions, farming is a remarkably robust way to describe Customer Success.

So think of Customer Success as farming your customers.

Your Customers Are Like Trees

I was born in a moshav in Israel, which is basically an agricultural village. My parents were farmers and we grew all sorts of stuff for a living. If you accept farming as a mental model for your business, I recommend raising metaphorical trees rather than perennials that die off every year.

I loved the smell of orange blossoms wafting from the trees on the Moshav, so let's think of your customers as orange trees. When you are growing orange trees, you have an innate understanding of their maturity stages— you need to do different things to them depending on their stage of growth in order to get the most oranges from your grove. Saplings require intensive care until they take root. Young trees have to be watered and fertilized differently than mature trees. When harvest time comes, the focus of activities shifts to harvesting. When you identify sick trees you have to move very quickly to nip disease in the bud. In addition, when you plant a tree you expect an annual yield from the tree over multiple years. The work is not a one-time effort and the tree is not a perishable asset.

Customer Success is about treating your customers like trees, nurturing them until they begin to yield a harvest, and then preserving them for as many seasons as possible.

YOUR GROVE IS YOUR BUSINESS

No single tree will make or break your season, rather it is the sum of profits from all of the trees that matters. Thus, you do need to monitor the overall health of your grove, with its many trees in various stages of maturity. This allows you to maximize its yield. And to do this you generally have to apply resources that are limited—your time, water, fertilizer and so on. You should prioritize your time and effort to ensure that no tree is left behind and that you're focused on every tree and on the grove performance (yield) overall.

In much the same way, implementing a program of Customer Success means managing your overall customer base and making choices about how to apply your limited resources to the segments of customers that will offer the greatest benefit to your business, both in terms of current and future revenue, all while ensuring that every customer is provided with appropriate value from your product. The prioritization of work required to do this effectively is a major challenge for all Customer Success organizations.

YOUR HARVEST IS YOUR REVENUE

Have you ever smelled orange blossoms? The scent means that the best time of year is coming – the harvest. Experienced farmers know in advance if the season is going to be great, normal, or disappointing. The predictability is a result of the work that has gone in over the course of the year and its impact on the trees; little can be done to improve the harvest by the time it actually rolls around.

If you have done your work well, meaning if you have prepared the ground, nurtured the seedlings and carefully nurtured your trees so that they will bear as much fruit as possible, you will have a bountiful crop.

And if you do the work of nurturing your customers correctly, so they are getting real ongoing value from your product – well, then that sort of success has a nice smell too.

THE GOAL

The point of all this is not necessarily to maximize your harvest in any one season—in fact, it can be counterproductive to do so. Rather, your goal is to maintain a healthy grove and ensure you can continue to harvest from it for years to come. This type of management often involves making tradeoffs between the long term and the short term, which need to be balanced carefully. Your goal as a farmer is to maximize the yield from your grove over time.

In terms of Customer Success, that balance and maximization is embodied in the concept of Customer Lifetime Value, or CLV.

CLV is the sum of the profit you make from your customers over time as opposed to a single upfront amount. Like an ongoing Profit and Loss statement on a per-customer level, the CLV takes into account how much the customer pays per year (value) less the costs of maintaining them per year (Customer Retention Costs or CRC) and the number of years during which they subscribe to the product.

The goal of Customer Success is to **PROACTIVELY IMPACT** CLV.

Chapter 3

The Customer Success Cycle (or, how your trees grow)

There are a few different stages in the lifecycle of your customers, and it behooves you to understand them. In particular, the old way of thinking of a customer funnel no longer applies to how your customers should be handled. The old funnel looked something like this:

Customers moved through the funnel predictably and were managed in lockstep by the sales and marketing team. Once the sale closed, there was little further concern for them other than to escalate complaints. But as I discussed earlier, the world has changed and that approach is no longer enough.

The new paradigm is more like this:

THE CUSTOMER SUCCESS CYCLE

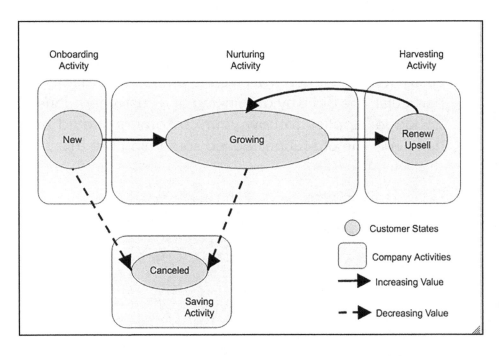

The key difference in this paradigm from the old one is that company activities have an effect on value in every stage of the customer lifecycle and the firm must remain engaged with the customer throughout. That engagement is basically Customer

Success. And there is no endpoint in this paradigm other than cancellation, a bad outcome.

It is worth explaining the details of this lifecycle and the company activities that correspond to it.

Customer States

New — This is the customer's state when they are newly signed. They have yet to derive value from the product, so in our tree metaphor they have yet to take root. During this stage the most important step is to get them to first value, so company activity focuses on what we call "Onboarding" or getting them set up.

Growing — This is the customer's normal status, and the stage in which they will ideally spend most of their time. In this stage value is created in part by the customer's use of the product and also by the firm through its "Nurturing" activities—everything from training to the introduction of new features. These activities all create increasing value designed to encourage new levels of engagement.

In Renewal/Upsell — While the Renewal or Upsell stages are short, they are important to both the customer and to you. What you do in these stages matters, but the outcome of the decision to renew or upsell comes mainly from lots of added value during the Growing stage. The activities the firm carries out during Renewal and Upsell must be focused not only on gathering revenue, but also on keeping and expanding the relationship. This is why I note the cycle between the Renewal/Upsell stage and the Growing stage—remember the goal is to keep customers in the Growing phase forever!

Cancelled — You will have churn and few activities will reverse it. Some attrition is impossible to avoid. But if this book does one thing it will help you lower that number by doing as much as possible during the New and Growing stages to add value for your customers and keep them with you.

Company Activities in Correlation to Customer States

Onboarding — All the work that takes place to get the customer from the New state to the Growing state, making sure they get to first value with the product.

Nurturing — Everything the company does for Growing customers to drive value, including things like training, introducing new use-cases and capabilities, performance reviews and so on.

Harvesting —Activities related to Harvesting include:

▶ **Renewing:** getting the customer to extend their existing contract

▶ **Upselling:** getting the customer to expand their existing contract

▶ **Cross-selling:** promoting different products to the same customer

Saving – The work done when you identify issues that may lead to customer cancellations.

I will describe each of these sets of activities in their own chapter in more detail.

THE CUSTOMER JOURNEY

Another way to visualize the path a customer travels in a subscription business is through the Customer Journey. The green line represents to optimal path of value progression for your customer that you would want them to take, while the yellow and red lines and sad faces represent challenges that the customer may experience during the journey that may result in customer cancellations.

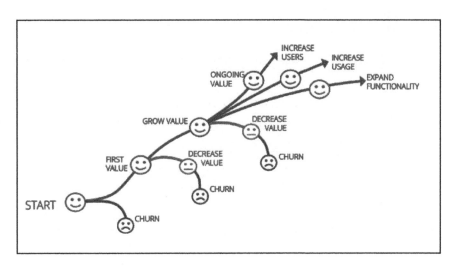

The Customer Journey is the customer's perspective of the Customer Success Cycle, which includes their view of the value they are getting and the actions they take as a result. The concepts are very similar—you need to understand the stage of development of your customers and take action to keep them on the right growth path.

WHERE THE FARMING METAPHOR BREAKS DOWN

There is an important caveat when it comes to the farming metaphor – and it follows directly from the Customer Journey idea I mentioned above. That caveat is the fact that your customers, unlike trees, have free will. They make the renewal, upsell and cancellation decisions. They have to cooperate with you during Onboarding and Nurturing. And they can decide to use or not use your product for any number of reasons that are completely out of your control. So it's worth having in mind not only where they are in the cycle, but also understanding in general terms what motivates customers to subscribe, renew/upsell, and cancel.

Subscription Motivations

Customers will **subscribe** for a variety of reasons:

▶ First and foremost for business reasons, to get business results from your product or service. A good way to train yourself and your team is that a subscription is always a 'trial' and it is the service provider's role to work with the client, making sure it delivers on the promise of results.

▶ For personal reasons, such as the fact that they used your product in a previous role, or they have a relationship with your company, or a friend recommended you.

▶ For strategic reasons, such as the need to move into a new market.

Additional reasons to subscribe can include other business, personal or unknown factors. Some motivations will be quantifiable, some will be strategic, and some emotional or relationship-based. It is crucial to understand the motivations of both the individual buyer and the buying organization. Regardless of the motivation, in a subscription environment your product will have to address those motivations consistently.

Renewal Motivations

A customer will **renew** if:

▶ The service has created ongoing value during the subscription term

▶ The company has become dependent on the service for one or more business use-cases

▶ The effort involved in canceling or switching to a new service is higher than the value of a replacement service.

Cancellation Motivations

Last, customers will **cancel** their subscription for as many reasons as they may have originally subscribed. Here is a very incomplete list:

▶ When the service has not provided value

▶ When the customer needs to cut costs or when they go out of business

▶ When the solution is not needed anymore

▶ When the solution was not adopted or fully deployed for a long period of time

▶ When there was no visibility into the value the product provided

▶ When leaders, buyers, users or decision makers leave the company

▶ When a better/cheaper/simpler/more reliable/ trendier alternative comes up

In fact, customers may even cancel if they feel that your product is good but they have a friend at a competing company! So, keep in mind that all of these motivations can affect your customers completely independently of everything you do to "farm" them. But you should still do all you can to nurture them.

Chapter 4

Managing Your Grove

Another way in which the farming metaphor is useful is that its lessons apply to both individual customers and at the aggregate level as well. In fact, your customer base is much like a grove of trees in how you must manage and work it.

Customer Success Is a Portfolio Management Exercise

When you manage segments of customers, some of them are New, most of them are at various Growing stages, some are in-renewal and some others are in danger of canceling. The goal is to make sure to maximize the value of the grove (the aggregate contract value over time) by successfully onboarding the New customers, continuously nurturing the Growing customers, managing escalations when those occur and maximizing renewal and upsell potential.

The challenge in doing this is focus and prioritization. Where to focus today, this week, this month, and this quarter in order to ensure a healthy grove which thrives and maximizes profit over time.

To successfully do that, you need to track customer status, health and various other key metrics that are state related in order to plan and execute an optimal plan that maximizes customer lifetime value across the entire portfolio of customers.

I would like to emphasize here that managing customer success is a portfolio management and optimization activity rather than a pipeline management, project management, or customer support management activity.

CUSTOMER SUCCESS VS. PIPELINE MANAGEMENT

New Customer Success organizations often model themselves on the classical sales process. The transaction is the renewal and for that reason they build a pipeline of renewals by looking at all the customers that are up for renewal in the next 45 or 90 days, etc.

The problem with this approach is that by the time a customer gets into the pipeline of renewals they have often already made the renewal decision. Your ability to actually influence their decision is reduced.

About early birds ...

Early on at Totango, we decided we needed a marketing automation system. We were about to launch our online product and we wanted a solution that would capture leads from our website. We signed up for a solution we liked.

Six months later our business was growing very quickly and we hired a marketing leader. She had a particular email marketing strategy in mind and didn't believe our then-current vendor could support it. So she signed us up for a different solution.

When the time came to renew the original contract, we canceled and the first vendor was surprised and upset. This taught me a good lesson – in many cases the renewal decision happens long before the renewal date.

CUSTOMER SUCCESS VS. PROJECT MANAGEMENT

Since the first stage of any Customer Success process is Onboarding, it seems easy to assume that Customer Success is about project management. Indeed, in many cases Onboarding is a project, with defined start and end events and a defined set of activities and timelines. However, once the onboarding project is over and the customer is live and growing, we still need to nurture them. That nurturing is made up of many recurring activities over time.

Customer Success vs. Customer Support

Many young Customer Success organizations are understaffed, dealing with incomplete products and huge customer expectations, which lead to a lot of customer escalations. As business leaders we all have heard the words of crisis: "the customer threatened to cancel..." and have taken part in the scramble that followed. In this model what triggers the activity and the rally behind the customer is the escalation. This is the basic pattern of customer support, one that Customer Success seeks specifically to avoid. Escalations are expensive, frustrating, and cannot be planned for. With customer success we do not want to react - we want to be proactive and make a positive impact long before escalation is needed by the customer. It's important to eliminate our reactive Customer Support mindset.

Remember, Customer Success isn't pipeline management, project management, or customer support. Think of it as a portfolio management and you will do well.

Focus on Drivers to Influence Outcomes

Renewals, upsell, and cancellations are outcomes. In order to influence the outcomes, we need to focus on the drivers that lead to those results. Most of the drivers that you can affect happen during the Onboarding and Nurturing stages. Thus, onboarding and nurturing customers successfully will most likely lead to renewals and upsell. Failed onboarding and insufficient nurturing in most cases will lead to escalations and cancellations.

If you are going to manage your grove correctly you need to track the right metrics. Luckily, technology enables you to track all different sorts of information about your trees in their various stages and cohorts. When you do, it is worth bearing in mind the difference between driver measures and outcome measures.

Drivers

Driver measures of Onboarding and Nurturing activity fall into a limited set of categories, and can have a positive or negative effect on outcomes.

Onboarding Drivers

1. **Onboarding complete** (positive effect): whether the customer is able to use the product.

2. **Time to Value** (positive or negative effect): the faster a customer onboards, the better.

3. **Initial Adoption** (positive effect): the rate at which individual users at the customer start using the product.

4. **Customer satisfaction** (positive effect): subjective yet quantifiable measures such as Net Promoter Score, which comes from a survey asking the customer whether they would recommend your product or service.

Nurturing Drivers

1. Adoption

1. **User Adoption** – daily use, monthly use rate, frequency of use.

2. **Feature Adoption** (positive effect): the percentage of your feature set that a customer or customer segment is using relative to those they are paying for. Again, a high number here is good and will often lead to improved renewal and upsell.

2. Capacity Utilization (positive effect): the percentage of the seats or licenses a customer or customer segment actually uses relative to those they are paying for. The higher this ratio the better.

3. Business Results (positive effect): the absolute or relative gains in whatever metric your customer or customer segment is trying to achieve. This might include sales leads for a sales automation system or new hires for recruiting software. In short, the tangible ROI that is delivered.

4. Operational Metrics

3. **Escalations** (negative or positive effect): the number, type, and time to resolution of inbound requests from customers. While a rule of thumb is that a lot of escalations correlate to higher churn, this is not always the case. When I discuss saving, I will cover the idea that the

time to resolution of escalations is an important mitigating factor.

4. **Payments** (negative or positive effect): how fast and reliably the customer pays.

5. **Customer Feedback** (positive effect): subjective yet quantifiable measures such as Net Promoter Score, which comes from a survey asking the customer whether they would recommend your product or service.

Outcomes

Recall that your goal in Customer Success is to positively impact Customer Lifetime Value. Since value in that context equals profit, your business goal is to maximize renewal and upsell while minimizing churn. Not coincidentally, those are the outcomes that you want to track:

1. **Renewals**: the dollar value and number of customers who extend their relationship with you.

2. **Upsell:** the dollar value and number of customers who expand their relationship with you.

3. **Churn:** the dollar value and number of customers who cancel or lapse their relationship with you.

As I mentioned earlier, these outcome measures are ultimately in the hands of your customer and reflect a decision already made by them. So if you want to preemptively impact CLV you need to try to influence drivers.

THE CUSTOMER SUCCESS SCORECARD (OR, YOUR GROVE REPORT CARD)

Once you have categorized your metrics into drivers and outcomes and divided them up by stage you are ready to create an overview of your entire customer base. I call this overview a Customer Success Scorecard, and it looks something like this:

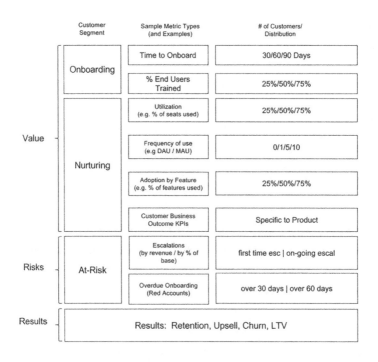

The key element in this scorecard is the far right column—Customer Distribution. In this column you will categorize all your accounts by the relevant metric. The list of metrics here is not exhaustive, but covers the main categories and provides and example for each. This categorization exercise will give you an overview of your entire customer landscape, sliced and diced by the drivers that affect your business outcomes. Creating these distributions has two effects:

1. You create a baseline of metrics on which to improve.

2. Skews in the distributions will immediately reveal driver metrics that need attention.

For example, if your Onboarding section shows that more than 50% of your customers are taking 60 days to complete Onboarding and 50% of those subsequently cancel then it is clear that you must take action to address the Time to Onboarding driver metric.

Chapter 5

Doing the Work

So far I've discussed the mental model for Customer Success and the information you want to monitor in order to understand what is happening with your customer base. Where the rubber really meets the road is with the work you and your team do to affect the drivers we've identified and ultimately change your outcomes – minimized churn and maximized renewals and upsells. As I mentioned earlier, the hard part for a Customer Success organization is to focus on the right activities for the right segment and prioritize the ones that will have the greatest impact on the Customer Success Scorecard. In practice this means an integrated process that includes the strategy, the tactics, and the customer engagement of the Customer Success organization.

Setting the Strategy

The leadership of the Customer Success organization sets up business goals derived from the company's goals that are annual, quarterly or monthly and operates in an execution cycle along the following lines:

1. **Planning** – Define the goals and priorities

2. **Tracking & Forecasting** – Current performance compared to the plan and goals in along with expected future performance for planning purposes

3. **Reporting & Analyzing** – communicate across the company the current performance and analyze reasons for those results.

THE TACTICS: ACTIVITIES OF A CUSTOMER SUCCESS MANAGER

It isn't as if the actual activities of Customer Success Managers are different from tasks native to other business contexts. They are simple to understand. I outline the main categories of activity, below, along with some examples as they might exist for a generic SaaS product.

The daily work Customer Success managers do can be roughly broken into work that is done independently of the customer before and after engaging, and work that is done with the customer, which we call engagement:

Customer Independent Activities:

These activities happen prior to and after customer engagements in order to ensure their work is impactful.

Preparing

- Preparing independently of the customer to understand the account and the business context.

- Working with the customer to establish short-term and long-term goals for the account and the relationship.

- Establishing milestones in support of account goals.

Analyzing

- Creating reports designed to inform management about account performance.

- Looking at customer and user data in order to develop hypotheses about use that can be reviewed with the customer.

Customer Engagement Activities:

These are the core activities of the CSM and are intended to drive value for the customer.

Setting up

- Provisioning new customer accounts.

- Configuring the accounts for use.

- Importing legacy data into the new product if required.

Training/Coaching

- Working with the customer to build the knowledge required to get value from the service.

- Introduce new capabilities that can drive further value.

- Doing product demonstrations.

- Guided use of the product with the customer.

- Using use cases to convey best practices.

Communicating

- Periodic interaction with the customer champion to review program status and activities.

- May also include management reviews on a weekly/bi-monthly/or monthly basis with customer executives in addition to the product champion depending on the depth of the engagement.

- Announcing to the customer product features or applications that may be useful for them.

- Sharing with the customer information about their use of the product and how it might improve.

Monitoring

- Keeping tabs on customer health indicators and taking action on any signals that fall outside the normal.

Reviewing

- Going over performance and usage with the customer.

- Presenting the results of analysis to the customer.

Solving

- Responding to complaints or requests from the customer.

- Finding and preempting problems which the customer may face before they ever raise them.

Driving

- In the absence of other pressing matters, finding ways to get the customer more engaged and for them to get more value.

The specifics of each activity can vary, depending the stage of the customer. For instance, training a new user will involve different emphasis than training an existing user.

The Engagement Model: Combining Activities into Success Programs and Success Plays

The way to affect drivers and ultimately outcomes is through what I call Success Programs and Success Plays.

Success Programs are ongoing sets of activities that repeat in time and across customers. Examples of Success Programs include Quarterly Business Reviews and New Feature Introductions, which happen periodically regardless of account status.

Success Plays are triggered sets of activities that your Customer Success team runs in response to a particular event. For instance, you can run a Success Play to counter a fall in usage, or to react to the departure of your product champion from your customer.

PUTTING IT ALL TOGETHER

Combining strategy, tactics, and the engagement model yields a process that looks something like the outline below. I use an annual planning cycle in this example, but feel free to swap in a time frame that matches your organization and goals.

1. **Business Goals** — Define a set of annual business outcomes:

    1. Attain 120% net retention by

    2. Upselling 50% of year 1 customers to adopting a higher tier package and 25% of year 2-5 customers adopting a higher tier package while

    3. Reducing churn by 2%

2. **Operating Plan** — Identify the drivers that should be targeted in order to meet those goals, for example:

    1. Successful onboarding within a maximum of 30 days

    2. Driving product adoption from 30% utilization on average to 50%

    3. Ensure 60% adoption of the product's stickiest feature

4. Reduce escalations from 30 a month to 20 a month by year-end

3. **Engagement Model** – Define the Success Programs and Success Plays that will influence the identified drivers:

   1. Success Programs

      1. Onboarding

      2. Training Program

      3. Adoption reporting Program

      4. Escalation reduction Program

   2. Success Plays

      1. Drive feature use for non-active users

      2. Ad-hoc training for low adoption accounts

      3. Target low usage users with communications campaigns

   3. Review the Customer Success Scorecard monthly for every cohort

   4. Review both the overall customer base and also break down by segment

   5. Broken down by Customer Success Manager

   6. Analyze the impact of the Success Programs and Plays and improve them as needed.

With this complete process you can see that there is a connection between what Customer Success managers do daily and the aggregate impact it exerts on the customer base.

THE IMPORTANCE OF INCREMENTAL AND ITERATIVE IMPROVEMENT

The modern B2B product environment is extremely complex, and it is not always clear how best to influence the system to improve outcomes. When you have this level of complexity, it is important to establish a process driven method of improvement.

I am a tremendous fan of the Agile Engineering model. If you are not an engineer you may not be familiar with it (and its scope is beyond my space here), but one of the fundamental insights from the model is the effectiveness of incremental and iterative improvement. In essence, create achievable goals based on your current baseline and adjust your methods as often as necessary to hit those goals.

At the heart of Agile is the assumption that there are unknowns about your business. The best way to improve our key performance indicators over time is by setting up short-term goals, planning to achieve those goals, and then measuring the outcomes. The process is repeated frequently with an eye for better execution patterns.

The application in the Customer Success context is that you should start with Success Plays that run on a 4,

8, or 12 week max cycle with clear goals of improving portfolios on their key metrics.

I cannot overstate how important this insight is when applied to Customer Success. All too often leaders set arbitrary top-down goals for outcome metrics such as a reduction in churn or an increase in upsell. I confess that I'm guilty of this myself!

But the whole point of establishing a Customer Success Scorecard and focusing on driver metrics is to achieve and exceed realistic goals, which should be the mindset of any organization. So if the baseline performance of your onboarding activity is that 30% of your accounts take longer than 60 days to onboard, your goal for the next quarter (12 weeks out) should be 20% (realistic), not 0% (unrealistic).

You get the point.

WHEN TO DO WHAT — PRIORITIZING THE STAGES

Generally speaking, it pays to build out your Customer Success capabilities roughly in line with the Customer Success Lifecycle. Here is a quick reminder of what that looks like.

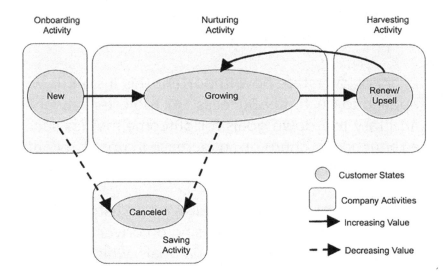

If your organization is completely new to Customer Success, you are most likely to be in a highly reactive mode, engaging with the customer only when they report a problem or threaten to cancel.

To get proactive, your first step should be to create a solid Onboarding process that creates a good experience from Day One for each of your customers.

Next, start developing your Nurturing processes to start generating the right levels of value for your customer, keeping them on the path to renewal and upsell.

Finally, focus on developing your Harvesting activities—the actual procedures you go through in order to Upsell customers who are near or at capacity and Renew those customers that have been getting value from the product over their cycle.

It goes without saying that as you are building out these capabilities, you should be doing what you can to streamline your Saving process and make it as efficient as possible. However, don't fall into the trap of spending all your resources on at-risk customers – both their value and your win ratio will tend to be low.

I'll discuss the specific Success Plays in each of these stages in the following chapters.

PRIORITIZING SUCCESS PLAYS WITHIN STAGES

The beauty of the Customer Success Scorecard with its metric-based segments is that it allows you to create scenarios that identify how you should prioritize your Success Plays. Here is the Scorecard again.

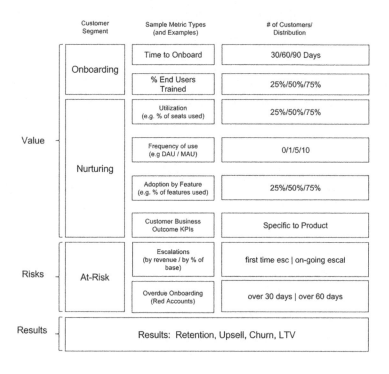

For example, let's say that you are looking at license utilization as a driver metric, and you find that your customers are distributed into 4 categories of license utilization.

- 20% of customers are at   < 20% utilization
- 50% of customers are at   < 21%-50% utilization
- 20% of customers are at   < 51-75 utilization
- 10% of customers are at   > 75% utilization

Moreover, you find that accounts that have <20% utilization at 60 days before renewal will churn 40% of the time.

Identify a segment of users that have <20% utilization per day at 60 days before renewal.

In keeping with the concept of incremental and iterative improvement, set the goal of lowering that driver metric from 20% to 15% in the coming 8 weeks, your next cycle.

You can quantify the effect of the accounts that move into the <21%-50% utilization segment and say the following:

"If I can decrease the size of the <20% utilization segment from 20% to 15% in the next quarter, this will result in $X of revenue saved to lower churn."

This allows you to compare the benefit of Success Plays deployed in support of this driver metric relative to the same effort devoted elsewhere.

Again, note that this is a bottom-up approach. It assumes the current distribution in the Customer Success Scorecard, targets an achievable incremental improvement in the driver metric, and compares that option against deploying resources to a different option.

ABOUT PLANNING AND PREDICTABILITY

As I've mentioned above, the goal of Customer Success is to proactively impact customer lifetime value or CLV. That means proactively impacting customer retention, growth and churn.

As the leader responsible for the revenue from all existing customers, the VP of Customer Success needs to plan for that impact and forecast the total revenue potential from retaining and growing those customers. She also needs to assess the amount of revenue that each type of customer generates. To achieve this it helps to understand what types of accounts have the best potential for growth.

Take a look at the following diagram. On the X axis customers are segmented by the dollar value they create for your business, and on the Y axis they are segmented by how much value they are deriving from your business.

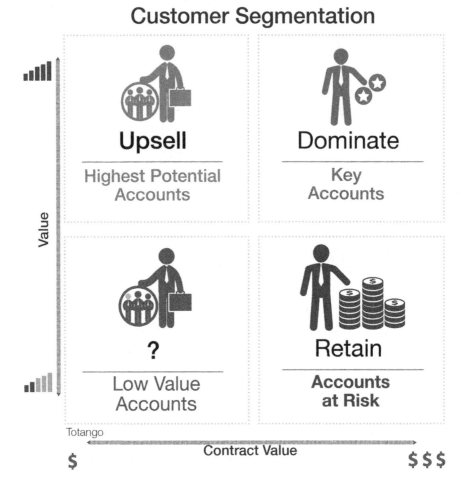

Customer Segmentation

As you can see, the groups that have a mismatch between the value to your business and the value they derive are the ones that demonstrate a clear and actionable potential.

By categorizing her accounts into this matrix, a Customer Success leader is able to better forecast her revenue and likely sources of potential growth.

Chapter 6:

Onboarding

There is no time when a tree is more vulnerable than when it has just germinated. A farmer understands this, and pays extremely close attention to newly germinated seedlings in their pans, making sure they have just the right amount of light, soil, and fertilizer so that they can be planted in the grove and start growing on their own. In Customer Success this vulnerable stage is called Onboarding.

Most Customer Success organizations separate Onboarding into its own stage for two reasons. First, it is clearly defined in terms of both time and functionality – customers are Onboarding until they can use the product on their own. Second, it is an extremely important phase on which to focus organizational attention because failure in the Onboarding phase means failure overall. The Onboarding stage is comprised of a single program, the Onboarding Program.

The goal of the Onboarding Program is to convert New customers into Growing customers while maintaining the sales momentum and excitement. In other words, to deliver quickly on the promise of value made by the Marketing and Sales teams to the customer during the sales process. If that doesn't happen, or doesn't happen quickly or effectively enough, then churn is likely to increase.

Let's assume your company sells an email marketing service, like Mailchimp. The Onboarding Program for your customers might look something like this:

THE CUSTOMER ONBOARDING PROGRAM

Goal:
Onboard new customers within 14 days (or the appropriate time for your business)

Metrics:

1. Time to onboard (to first value)

2. Customer satisfaction post onboarding

3. Initial Value and Product adoption

Segments:

New Customers

Activities:

1. Kick off call – define the goal, scope, timeline, and key milestones of the onboarding project.

2. Technical Setup – provision the system for the customer, provision new users, import data, and so on.

3. Business setup and configuration – configure the system (if needed) to support the customer use case.

4. Training – coach and train the customer and the key users on how to use the system to meet their business goals. Provide first-time tips and tricks and smooth the initial adoption.

5. Kick-off review via a call or in-person meeting.

If any one of the steps in the Onboarding Program is not completed, then you could run a Success Play to address it. Below are some situations that might occur:

CUSTOMER ONBOARDING SUCCESS PLAYS

Trigger: The customer is unable to use the product

The CSM View:
Mike, a CSM at an email marketing software company, logs into his workstation on Tuesday morning. In his queue of activities for the day he notices a flashing red task: apparently there are three users at a major client who have had multiple unsuccessful logins. No one has called, but Mike suspects their user accounts might not have been configured properly.

Success Play: Troubleshooting onboarding

1. Setup as necessary. The CSM must configure the back end of the product and make any connections necessary via APIs or other methods and transfer legacy data into the new system. To do that, the Customer Success team needs to learn the customer's current technical context in order to correctly set up the system and transfer any legacy data into the new product. When the technical setup is complete a transaction should occur, which confirms the setup. The CSM should also confirm with the customer via email or phone that setup is complete. This step can be (and in many cases is) automated.

2. Additional training for the customer to use the product. The CSM should base their training on the customer's context and make it specific to solving their business problem. Whether live, via a conference call/screen-share or an automated guided tour, the CSM should ensure the customer has the knowledge needed to be able to effectively use the features necessary for their business goals. After training, CSM should follow up with the customer to ensure the training was sufficient and appropriate.

3. Communicate via an email campaign. First the CSM should generate a segment of accounts or users that are below a baseline of usage frequency. Then she should review the accounts and see if they had any elements in common. Some things to keep an eye out for might include, but are certainly not limited to:

▶ Are there notes in the account that point to difficulties?

▶ When were the accounts created?

▶ What was the last feature the customer used?

▶ Who was the salesperson on the account?

For instance, if many of the low-usage accounts seem to have gotten stuck on a particular feature, the email should include a reference to that feature and offer assistance in using it.

With Success Plays, the point of the activity is not the internal measure—"Did I send the email?" but rather the customer measure—"Did the customer accelerate or expand their use of the service?" If the answer to the latter question is "No," then the Success Play has not succeeded. Not only should the CSM try something else, but also they should log the low effectiveness of the play so that it is not repeated in the future.

Trigger: The customer is unhappy with the onboarding process

The CSM View:
Venkash, a Director of Customer Success and Mike's boss, receives a notification that several users on a major account have logged low Net Promoter Scores. While a low score is not itself a cause for success, several low scores from the same large client set off a yellow Health Indicator. Venkash calls over Mike, the CSM on the account, to find out why the customer might be unhappy.]

Success Play: Follow up with the customer

1. Analyze customer data prior to contact. More than with any other Success Play, an outbound phone call requires real research to understand the customer's situation and their likely problems. The worst thing a CSM can do is call a dissatisfied customer and waste their time! So, at minimum, the CSM must know the following:

   ▶ The specific people at the firm with whom the customer has interacted—personal chemistry is the source of much, if not most, dissatisfaction in the Onboarding period.

   ▶ The customer's specific business problem and how the product was intended to fix it—in other words, the promise that was made by Sales and Marketing.

   ▶ The usage pattern, not only of the main contact at the customer, but of the user base overall. This means understanding which features are being used and which are not used.

   Only with all this knowledge is the CSM ready to reach out to the dissatisfied customer. The call should open with some kind of insight—"I reviewed your account and found that you could be saving three hours a week by..." Once this value has been conveyed, the CSM can begin probing for the reasons behind the low NPS.

2. Communicate via an outbound phone call. The goal of an outbound phone call is to provide value to your dissatisfied (or under-utilizing) customer

by telling them something that they don't know, which is useful to them.

NPS surveys are not fielded daily or, ideally, even weekly. But to the extent that they are built into the product, they should be monitored for improving or declining trends. In the instance when the CSM has already done an outbound phone call to investigate a low NPS, there should be to-do items, which should be followed up on and conveyed to the customer when fixed.

SPECIAL TOPIC: CUSTOMER HEALTH INDICATORS

An important part of setup in the Onboarding stage is the establishment of Health Indicators. One of the best methods for monitoring the status of a customer, a Health Indicator establishes baseline performance for a set of relevant metrics and then indexes that number to three states: green for healthy, yellow for in danger, and red for crisis.

In the case of our email marketing service, we might consider creating a combined metric out of logins per month, emails sent per user, and amount of storage used per user. The initial level of the index is less important than the process of calibrating the index and tracking it over time.

Chapter 7:

Nurturing

Farmers spend most of their time caring for healthy, growing trees to ensure a successful season and a plentiful harvest. They water them regularly and monitor them directly for signs that they are healthy and are getting enough nutrients and light. They sometimes guide their growth with stakes or strings. They also make sure that the trees don't show signs of disease.

This concept is worth emphasizing: *most of your time is spent nurturing customers in the Growing stage of their Customer Success Cycle.* This is true from both an effort standpoint as well as from **a time one**. In fact, on a standard 12 month recurring revenue cycle, over 80% of the activity falls into Nurturing, as we see in the following:

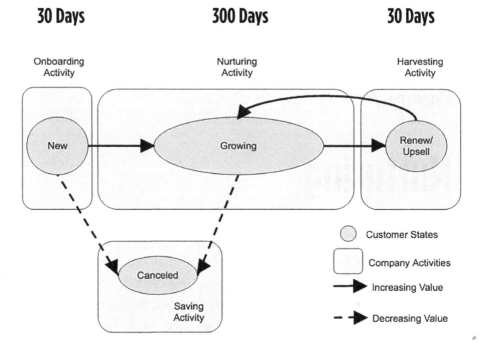

Nurturing Growing customers is a mix of ongoing Success Programs, as well as constant monitoring and applying Success Plays when meaningful events are identified.

NURTURING SUCCESS PROGRAMS

Nurturing Success Programs are targeted to all Growing customers, or specific segments in order to achieve a business goal. Much like a farmer waters the grove twice a week, these are sets of repeated processes designed to ensure the health of Growing customers.

A typical Success Program has the following characteristics:

1. A Goal

2. Metrics by which to measure the outcomes of the program

3. A target customer segment

4. Key activities

Below you can find common Nurturing Success Programs:

Feature Adoption Program

Goal:
Drive adoption of a specific feature. This may be because the feature is newly introduced. Or, sometimes it is important to emphasize the feature that drives the most value to differentiate your service from the competition.

Metrics:
Usage volume of the target feature

Segment:
Growing customers that are not using this feature

Sample Activities:

1. Communicating the benefits of the feature via an outbound campaign.

2. Training on the feature via a weekly webinar that describes the use of the feature and its benefits.

3. Driving adoption of the feature via CSM phone or email outreach.

In a modern service delivery organization, new functionality is being introduced all the time. This Success Program ties directly to the service release timeline and is often closely coordinated with the product management and product marketing organizations.

I recently came across an example of a successful feature adoption program by an email marketing SaaS company. The firm had invested a lot in building simple reporting and analytics capabilities. It had also learned that customers who used the analytics feature were less likely to cancel their subscription. On this basis the VP of Customer Success decided to make sure that every customer that had been using the product for over 3 months should learn how to take advantage of the analytics feature. So he built an Analytics Adoption Program, pushing the analytics feature using a variety of methods. Within 3 months he was able to double the adoption of this feature.

Usage Reporting Program

Goal:
To communicate to the customer the value that the product or service has provided to their organization during the period.

Metrics:
1. License Utilization

2. Daily Active Users

Segment:

All Growing Stage customers

Sample Activities:

1. Communicate with the customer via a weekly report that summarizes the last week's usage, trends, and value being delivered and suggest potential growth opportunities.

Note: this program does not necessarily require CSM involvement and could be fully automated. That said, if it is automated it should still be configured to present the usage data most relevant to the customer.

Periodic Business Review Program

Goal:

To make sure customers understand the value delivered by the service and align partnership goals and plans.

Metrics:

1. Composite customer health indicators as discussed in Chapter 6

2. Usage metrics

3. Feature adoption metrics

Segment:

Growing customers who have been determined to be high value and high priority

Key Activities:

1. Schedule a periodic business review with stake-holders from the customer.

2. Prepare and review collateral to discuss with the customer.

3. Meet and share information. After the meeting, document the discussion, commitments and customer sentiment.

4. Follow up on action items from the review.

Customer Feedback Program

Goals:

1. To get customer feedback and identify potentially dissatisfied customers.

2. To learn from trends in feedback whether the nurturing programs are driving improvement that is reflected in improved customer satisfaction.

Metrics:

1. Customer feedback score

2. Net Promoter Score

Segment:
All growing customers that do not have escalations

Key Activities:

1. Track customer feedback via a survey.

2. Analyze the survey results and extract positive or negative trends.

3. Review status with those customers that had negative feedback and address their concerns.

Best Practice Sharing Program

Goal:
To drive wide adoption of successful use-cases within the customer base.

Metrics:

1. Feature adoption

2. Utilization

Segment:
Growing customers that have reached first value and are ready for advanced use-cases based on their maturity and needs.

Key Activities:

1. Train via a monthly webinar featuring a customer that shares their use case and lessons learned.

2. Communicate via weekly email campaigns that communicates use-case per week.

Nurturing Success Plays

Whereas Nurturing Programs tend to run on a schedule and are initiated by the Customer Success Organization, Nurturing Success Plays are event-based and are triggered by customer behavior. By monitoring customer vital signs, the Customer Success organization is able to identify leading indicators of negative outcomes and engage in time to prevent them.

Below, I review some common Success Plays that come up during the Nurturing stage in many recurring revenue businesses.

Trigger: Account Suffers from a Drop in Utilization

Success Play: Investigate usage with the customer

1. Touch base with key contacts at the customer.

2. Learn what changes that led to the drop in usage.

3. Address the issues discovered. These might include a training a new team at the customer, or changing the product configuration to reflect a shift in the customer's business priorities, or any number of other reasons.

4. Document the incident and the response.

5. Track whether the changes implemented lead to improved utilization.

Note: there could be many reasons why account turns red or even yellow (see the Special Topic on Health Indicators in Chapter 6). The key is to identify the change and the reason behind the change in order to take appropriate measures.

Trigger: Users Affected by a Service Outage or SLA Breach

In this example, a key function of the service was not working properly for some time and several users were affected.

Success Play: Act preemptively to make up for a bad experience

1. Once the issue has been resolved, identify the users that were impacted.

2. Communicate with those users immediately and acknowledge the issue.

3. Create a reward or incentive to compensate them for the issue.

Case Study:

One of Totango's telecommunications clients, a business services company, routinely used this Success Play when their customers went over capacity and had a bad experience. By reaching out to those customers before they even called in, our client was able offer them a solution to their problem that often included purchasing further capacity. By proactively engaging the customer to address a potential problem they not only averted an escalation, but often benefited from an upsell as well.

Trigger: A Key User Leaves the Company

Your champion, the user who uses your product most often, does not log in for over a week. It turns out he found a new job.

Success Play: Re-establish engagement with the customer

1. Reach out to other people at the customer in order to re-establish a key connection.

2. Identify a new champion and ensure they are engaged with the product.

3. Reach out to your old champion, determine his new role, and pass the lead on to the Sales team.

Trigger: A Support Storm – Many Similar Cases Occur

Success Play: Learn from early incidents and apply lessons to the entire customer base

1. Escalate the issue internally.

2. Run a problem-solving routine with the customer even if the customer did not request it.

3. Resolve any issues uncovered by the internal or customer investigation

4. Follow up to make sure the issue does not recur.

Often in a Customer Success environment, it is necessary to use the learning from a single case to fix a problem that has occurred across the entire customer base. By being proactive and connecting the dots when multiple similar cases occur, you will be able to exceed customer expectations by solving their problems before they escalate.

Trigger: Slow Ramp Up in Use After Onboarding

Individual users or the account as a whole can experience below normal growth in engagement with the product. When this happens, the corresponding Success Play is designed to figure out the issue and address it.

Success Play: Troubleshoot usage ramp up with the customer

1. Communicate with the customer and figure out if the use pattern is appropriate.

2. If slow ramp represents a training issue, arrange for training.

3. If end users seem unaware of features or functionality, arrange outbound communication or training.

4. Follow up to make sure usage grows more quickly.

Trigger: Customer is Not Seeing Business Results

Ultimately your customer measures their results based on their own business context. They signed up for and are using your product not because they like it but because it will do something for them.

So the number of logins, the number of features used, and the number of users are ultimately just a proxy for whether the customer is seeing business results. And in the case of many products, you can measure their business results directly.

Let's take the case of a lead generation product, a plat-form designed to generate more leads per time than their previous system. This metric would not only have been a key part of the sales and marketing process—in fact the very basis for the promise of your product—it should also have become a Health Indicator all on its own.

If the Business Results metric is flashing red you have a serious problem.

Success Play: Troubleshoot lagging business results

1. Analyze customer data to narrow down the problem.

2. If customer data does not reveal the issue, communicate with the customer to understand whether they are using the product correctly or enough.

3. Arrange Onboarding if appropriate.

4. If all users have been onboarded, consider training on best practices.

5. Continue to troubleshoot until business results metrics improve.

CASE STUDY: DO AS I SAY, NOT AS I DO!

In 2013 Totango was flying high. It had acquired over 60 customers for its SaaS platform to manage Customer Success. Like many startups in its situation, Totango had grown quickly and still had a small team with few processes. In an unexpected and somewhat ironic turn of events, the company was hit with a churn problem in 2014. Though it often advised its own clients to pay close attention to their churn figures, we seemed to be stuck fighting our own rear guard battle, losing several customers each quarter in a string of surprises that was notable because there seemed little the company could do to stem the tide. Each departing customer was like a breakup, with a strong impact on company morale. Importantly, resources that might have been devoted maintaining high value customers in the high-value quadrant were diverted to trying to save customers in the high-risk quadrant

So, in 2014, we made a key decision to sacrifice two quarters worth of growth and write off customers that were at risk, focusing on nurturing those which had high value and whose outcomes we could affect. The decision was widely contested at the company, but with the resources freed by the move we were able to implement a "play to win strategy." Under this strategy the company focused not on saving unhappy customers, but on doubling down on making already happy customers even happier and allowing the rest to churn. From this base, CSMs began working on really delivering value and figuring out ways to delight their customers. After several months of retooling, the company restarted on its growth path to stellar results in 2015 marked by a negligible churn figure.

An important lesson that I've learned: sometimes you have to break down the reactive cycle by making a tough decision and an aggressive move to a proactive mode of operation.

CHAPTER 8:

Harvesting

After much time, care, and resources have been invested, a farmer's crop is finally ready for gathering. Now is not the time for her to sit back and relax! In fact, harvest time can be the busiest time of the year, a time when badly assigned or executed work will most directly lead to lost yield. So, during harvest time a farmer uses different techniques and often brings in specialist workers to gather the crop.

In a highly competitive environment, the rate at which you renew and upsell affects both the speed at which you grow and the size that you can achieve. Yet many companies are more focused on new user acquisition than on a well-managed renewal and upsell process, to their detriment. In fact, a recent survey from Pacific Crest Partners showed that small SaaS companies of less than $1.25MM in Annual Recurring Revenue (ARR) rely on upsells for only 11% of their sales, while large ones (greater than $40MM in annual revenue) rely on upsells for 30% of their revenue. While this may seem intuitive, it is not a license for small companies to delay focusing on optimizing their Renewal and Upsell process. On the contrary, small SaaS firms that had the highest portion of their revenue from upsells grew the fastest, as well.

The CSM View:
Every month Mike and the other CSMs on his team sit down to review their Renewal pipeline. Today they are looking at the accounts that will be renewing in 90 days. Though this is quite far out, they know that if there are serious issues they have to jump on them now. Sure enough, Mike notices that two of his accounts have escalations that are quite old. He checks into them and realizes that they are product requests that have not yet been added to the development queue. Knowing that just keeping them posted can make a difference, Mike takes a note to check with the Engineering team so that he can communicate an update to those customers.

Because Renewal happens on a regular basis we treat it as a Success Program.

HARVESTING SUCCESS PROGRAM

Goal:
To get the customer to extend their contract.

Key Metrics:

1. Renewal

2. Outstanding escalations

Key Activities:

1. Review the account and create an action plan for renewal starting well before the customer has to make the decision. If your organization is mature enough to afford it, you should assign these commercial activities to someone other than the CSM. I discuss this division of labor in greater detail in the chapter on building your team.

2. Communicate via a Renewal Audit. In preparation for this meeting, the CSMs should review information pertinent to their accounts. Such information should come from anyone in the firm who has interacted with the account and cover business performance, commercial issues, and escalations. This preparation should yield an estimate of the likelihood that each customer in the pipeline will renew. To the extent that specific accounts present a problem, the meeting should result in specific assignments to fix those problems with enough time to increase renewal likelihood.

3. Drive Renewal with a Renewal Plan. Based on the customer's current utilization and usage metrics, the CSM should document the steps that the firm and the customer will take in the lead up to renewing the contract. These may include any or all of further training, upgrades, escalation resolution, or personnel changes requested by the customer.

Unlike Renewals, Upsell and Cross-Sell opportunities can arise at any time and are triggered by customer behavior, so we treat them as Success Plays.

Harvesting Success Plays

Trigger: Account Approaching Utilization Capacity

The CSM View:
Many of the reminders in Mike's Customer Success software indicate some kind of a problem. But not all of them. The best reminders are the ones that show that one of his accounts is ripe for an Upsell or a Cross-Sell. This is partly because Mike gets a bonus when customers expand their usage. But more importantly it means that they are really using the product and getting value from it. Of course, Mike and his clients have been reviewing their usage so consistently that nearing capacity isn't really a surprise. In fact just last week on his monthly call with a client Mike pointed out that they were using the product so much they would hit cap soon – the client knew already.

Upsell and Cross-sell are not timeline-based, but rather a function of the customer approaching full capacity utilization. In a previous chapter I discussed Success Plays designed to increase utilization when it lags. In the positive situation that utilization exceeds quota, you should run an Upsell/Cross-Sell Success Play.

Success Play: Outbound Upsell/ Cross-Sell Communication

Key Metrics

1. Capacity utilization (seats)

2. Usage metrics (features)

Activities:

1. Review both the frequency and depth of product use, not only by the product champion but by everyone in his organization. An outbound upsell campaign is appropriate when you have launched a new feature or product that can lead to an Upsell/Cross-Sell opportunity.

2. It is important that the Upsell opportunity that results from the customer increasing usage over time should not be a one-off campaign, but rather an outcome of the ongoing review of customer usage. To be most effective, the Upsell/Cross-Sell communication should be part of the regular cadence of reviews with the customer (whether in person or automated) as the CSM reviews with the customer their usage and suggests actions based on it. This way, the suggestion to increase the contract is natural to the customer and does not feel like an opportunistic selling activity by the vendor.

3. The management of the Upsell/Cross-Sell transaction should fall to someone other than the point-of-contact CSM in order to separate the commercial relationship from the advisory one.

Note that if a customer accepts an Upsell offer they have effectively entered the New stage once again. They will require a comparably diligent level of Onboarding and

Nurturing for the expanded functionality or expanded user base.

Chapter 9:

Saving

Your trees will sometimes get sick. It can happen for any number of reasons. In the best case you will know what signs to look for and take action to prevent further damage before the tree's yield is affected. But once it starts to show symptoms you really, really need to act. Or, when you recognize symptoms of something incurable, you have to be ruthless about cutting it down.

Think of the quintessential subscription business: your cable provider. Regardless of where you live, your cable provider is probably one of the most loathed companies in your area. Its monopoly power has allowed it to avoid the churn inherent in other recurring revenue businesses. In particular, problems are solved only after much delay and inconvenience, and the primary method of preventing cancellations is erecting barriers to exit rather than providing a great service.

While cable companies run a subscription-based business, they do not have real churn risk. Conversely, most subscription businesses are not monopolies and have inherent churn risks as their customers have choice and can decide to take their business elsewhere pretty easily.

The ideal way to prevent churn is to excel at escalations to the point that you escalate internally before the customer even knows they have a problem. Think of the Internal Renewal Assessment Success Play. The point of that play is to identify issues before they become issues in the renewal process and fix them, to the customer's delight.

While the typical cable TV company is unfortunately a good example of what not do to, let's look at an example worth emulating: your favorite bartender. Bar owners know that a good bartender is vital to the success of their business. They know their customers and they use that knowledge of what those customers want and don't want to keep them coming back night after night.

Like the best bartender in the city, your goal is to monitor digital signals from your customers and anticipate their needs and offer them a solution at exactly the right moment – in fact, this is the exact concept of a Success Play I've been discussing.

To take the bartending metaphor a step or two further, think of your favorite bartender – not only do they know your drink preference (business needs), but they also know when to leave you alone.

**A Good Bartender Knowns
Exactly When to Ask About Refill**

They are discreet when they notice your glass is nearing empty, a raised eyebrow is the only inquiry they need to make of you. They know you well enough that they disappear when you want to be alone and yet are there to talk you through your problems when you are disposed to share. They **preact** based on the signals you send, signals you often don't even know yourself.

In a digital context the signals given off by your customers can be very subtle. I often use the example of Amazon to illustrate this point. A few months back my family and I were watching Inside Out on Amazon Prime (great movie, by the way, you should watch it.)

The morning after I rented the movie, I had an email in my inbox from Amazon that told me that despite the fact that I had paid for an HD version, network problems had forced them to show standard definition for part of the movie. And they offered me a free movie to make up for it.

Talk about preempting a problem! I didn't even notice the issue, but they did. Which is the perfect illustration of what is possible when delivering a digital product— you can know as much, or more than, your customers, and can preempt issues in a way that makes the experience delightful.

The alternative, that of treating me like a cable subscriber, just won't fly in the real world.

So, let's avoid that! When it comes to at-risk customers that you have to save, you should consider the following Success Plays.

All about selling

In 2009 I was pitching Totango and customer success technology to an ex-CEO of a public and very successful software company who was still selling its product as a one-time license for hundreds of thousands of dollars. After listening politely, the CEO said "Guy, even though anyone who hears your presentation will *say* that they have their customer's best interest in mind, the truth is that we make money by selling. Everything else, whether support, or services or whatever...we do it, but none of it is as important for us as selling."

SAVING SUCCESS PLAYS

If it takes you a long time to fix your customer's problems then you will lose them. The only question is how long it will take. So, when you discover a segment of customers with outstanding escalations you should pay close attention. Since escalations are by definition reactive and by definition triggered by customer behavior, we address them with Success Plays.

Trigger: Too Many Escalations

Some customers are problem customers and complain a lot. But, on the assumption that the majority of the complaints are reasonable, a large number of complaints per time can indicate performance issues on your part, miscommunication, or a mismatch between your product and their needs. You need to find out which and take the necessary steps to fix the problem.

Success Play: Internal investigation

1. The CSM should review the customer or customer segment escalations to discover if there are common issues that require internal resolution. There may be chronic commercial problems, which require Finance to change their workflow, or chronic Product problems, which should be addressed in the next development sprint on common technical issues worthy of a special effort to address outside the normal release cycle.

2. Once identified, the CSM should convey the information and justifications to the necessary team(s). Once your team has a clear mandate for a fix, they should pass it on with as much supporting evidence as possible.

It is not enough to pass on a request! The role of the Customer Success team is to be the advocate for the customer within the organization. This means following up on requests for internal changes, seeing them through to completion, and conveying success to the customer.

Hidden churn

Early on in its development, even that superstar of SaaS, Salesforce, had a major churn problem. They were growing so fast that it was not a major concern for management until one particular management offsite, when the topic came up almost incidentally.

During that meeting, someone put up a slide that showed the company was losing 2-3% of its customers per month. Cumulatively this was a huge drag on growth, north of 30% per year. It took Salesforce creating a special taskforce to focus on the churn problem to get it under control.

Chapter 10:

Building the Team

Customer Success has been implemented in many different ways at successful recurring revenue companies. The group can and has reported to the Chief Revenue Officer, the Chief Marketing Officer, and to the CEO. Still, there are a lot of teams reporting to the VP Sales and or VP of Operations. I strongly believe that the most effective positioning is a CEO reporting relationship in the form of a Chief Customer Officer or VP of Customer Success. All customer-touching roles should report in to this executive.

From a practical standpoint your first action as a leader implementing a Customer Success program is to assign Customer Success-related duties to someone in your organization. In the best case you will grow quickly enough to justify hiring a fully dedicated Customer Success resource soon. Regardless, you will have to consider several aspects of building your Customer Success team as you grow.

As is the case with all the lessons in this book, the structure, roles, and responsibilities of your Customer

Success Team flow from the Customer Success Cycle. In particular, whether you have a single CSM doing it all or a highly specialized group, your Customer Success team will have to carry out the following day-to-day activities that correspond closely to the Success Programs and Success Plays I have discussed in earlier chapters:

1. **Onboarding** – Get the customer live.

2. **Relationship Management** – Manage the customer interaction.

3. **Analysis and Reporting** – Monitor customer health.

4. **Commercial Management** – Manage the commercial outcomes, including renewals, upsells, cross sells and more.

5. **Knowledge Management** – Instruct the customer on the use of the product and ensure they are up to date on relevant information.

6. **Technical Support** — Troubleshoot escalations and liaison with Product and other functions.

On Day One your Customer Success team must do all these things. But very quickly you will need to specialize these functions by role. On the next page you will find detailed descriptions of each role.

Customer Success Manager (CSM).

This is your first Customer Success hire, made even before the hire of a more senior Customer Success VP.

The CSM is the lifeblood of your Customer Success team. As the CEO of the account, the CSM should be aware of every engagement the account has with every other role on the Customer Success Team.

I have found that the personality traits required for a successful CSM involve a hybrid of several functional backgrounds. Each has its own strengths and weaknesses. These tend to correlate to the various mental models of Customer Success I described in the "Managing Your Grove" chapter. For example, if a CSM comes from a Sales background, they might think in terms of a pipeline, reaching out to accounts too often. On the plus side, such a background has a relationship focus and a revenue focus that can be quite valuable. A different background, that of the Customer Support rep, can be valuable because these hires are often great at problem solving. The trade-off is that they tend to be reactive and wait until problems arise, rather than fixing problems and finding solutions before the customer knows they need anything. Project managers, with their deep technical and organizational skills, can be of great value in getting customers engaged with the platform and the handling of detail. Yet they often lack the relationship skills of salespeople and customer support backgrounds.

The ideal CSM takes the best of all these roles and uses them to farm. They are revenue motivated but have a light touch. They are highly relationship driven and work for the long term. They are proactive and sensitive to customer needs. They understand the product inside-out in order to help drive customer adoption. And last, they have in-depth domain knowledge gathered from multiple customers in the same vertical that makes them a highly valuable source of advice.

The strategy for you as a hiring manager is to keep these relative strengths in mind as you hire, and when you hire from a particular background, make sure that the other aspects you seek are either there or are trainable in the person you hire for the role. I have read hundreds of role descriptions for CSMs in my time, and most boil down to a basic set of responsibilities and requirements, which align closely to the activities I mentioned earlier.

Common Responsibilities

- Onboard new customers.

- Become a trusted advisor to multiple people in the account and become the account's advocate within the company.

- Build relationships with a network of champions within the account.

- Teach client to be self-sufficient within the service to influence technology adoption.

- Manage escalations from the client quickly and effectively.

- Run reports for management and for the client.

Common Requirements

- 3 years experience
- Relationship-focused
- Ability to teach
- Detail-oriented
- Team-player

Support Manager

As soon as you are able, you should break out Support from the CSMs activities.

I am often asked what the difference is between Customer Support and Customer Success. In my mind it's clear – a support person manages a queue of technical tickets and is not assigned to a particular account. They are technical in focus, as opposed to a CSM, who is concerned with the customer's business.

From this follows the ideal character of the support person. She is technical and well versed in product. She is good at problem solving within the company, seeking out the source of reported problems, whether technical or otherwise, and finding ways to fix them. She has high throughput and is extremely detail oriented.

Education Manager – Training Manager

My view on the education function is slightly controversial. As a company grows its customer base and the complexity of its product grows as well, it becomes more and more necessary to have specialized educators on hand. And I believe that it is they, not marketing, who should create the learning content required to ensure the customer gets the full value from an evolving product.

These trainers are concerned with both content creation and the logistics of training itself, from producing webinars and learning materials to actually doing new user training.

They are also key sources of the knowledge that will be needed for Self-Success, automating those tasks which have been done by CMS so as to make the team more scalable.

I've been asked how this role is different from that of the CSM. While it is true the CSM does a lot of training, she does not have a lot of time for content creation. And the focus of such content is different when targeted at existing customers than when it is targeted at the market more broadly, which is when it is produced by Marketing.

So, this role requires the ability to synthesize and explain complex concepts. It requires a desire to teach and a great degree of patience.

Operations Manager

As is the case with other functional Operations teams like Sales Ops and Marketing Ops, the Customer Success Ops team maintains the technology necessary for the Customer Success team.

The Operations team is also responsible for running analytics for the CSMs, providing them with metrics on the performance of their accounts and also providing management with metrics on the performance of the CSMs.

The Customer Success Operations manager or someone on the operations team also tends to be the Data Analyst, charged with understanding the customer base through analysis of the whole range of data the company acquires about those customers.

Upsell/Renewals Manager

When your Customer Success team is handling enough accounts that it can support further specialization, the commercial aspect of Renewals and Upsells should be managed by specialists. The reason for this distinction is that the CSM should be viewed as a trusted advisor by the customer. They should not be perceived to be trying to constantly sell.

Professional Services

On some level many of the services provided by the other roles in Customer Success are bundled into the

Professional Services category. The only difference is that Professional Services provides those services at price. This model is more common among SaaS businesses that target the Enterprise segment, with its more time-intensive implementation requirements.

You should think of your professional services team as a mini-version of your overall Customer Success team, with specialties in Onboarding, Relationship Management, Training, and Support. Excluded from their role are Renewal and Upsell and Encouraging Advocacy.

CUSTOMER SUCCESS RELATIVE TO OTHER BUSINESS FUNCTIONS

It's worth taking a moment to discuss how these Customer Success team members interact with other functions, because if I haven't made it clear by now, it is of crucial importance to deploy Customer Success thinking and responsibilities throughout the organization.

Sales

Customer Success is a revenue function, not a cost center. Yet CEOs have historically and continue to prioritize Sales activity – new customer acquisition – over existing customer retention and upsell. This is a mistake. From the standpoint of ROI, there is extensive data that shows that revenue is much cheaper to grow by investing in existing customers.

Also, the fact that Customer Success is a revenue function means that some portion of the compensation for CSMs needs to be variable and a function of revenue. Initially, CSMs who cover multiple Customer Success activities should have Renewal and Upsell as part of their responsibilities.

Over time, however, Renewal and Upsell should be a specialized commercial function within the Customer Success group, overseen not by the Head of Sales, but by the Head of Customer Success.

By the way, the way to maximize the output of your farm is to plant the healthiest and most appropriate plants in the first place. This is why the Customer Success executive should be reviewing the deals in the prospect pipeline with the Sales team on a regular basis, using the data of the CS team to identify those prospects that don't really fit the model, that have a higher risk of churn – and then seeing what could be done to make that risky deal more solid. And if it can't be improved, don't close it.

Customer Support

If Customer Success has a C-Level executive to lead it, as I recommend, the Chief Customer Officer will also oversee the Support Team.

As I mention in the role description for support personnel, support needs to keep the CSM apprised of all of the actions it is taking relative to a particular account.

Plus, if Success and Support are part of the same team, it's much easier to dynamically allocate people and resources between them depending on business conditions.

Product

While it is perhaps counterintuitive that Customer Success should have a close working relationship with the Product team, this is absolutely the case. Because Customer Success is highly attuned to how value is being created (or not) for the customer, having a tight feedback loop into the Product roadmap is essential. As a bare minimum, CSMs should participate in feature planning sessions. More formally, the product ticketing queue should include a Customer Success track for features that need to be prioritized.

If you think about it, the Sales function never hesitates to communicate to Product that if they just add a particular feature then Sales could close a huge deal – though it doesn't always turn out that way. The cost of those extra features can be substantial in terms of the breakage that inevitably occurs to other functions in the process.

While I do not advocate Customer Success similarly requesting an endless number of features, as a function they are so close to the customer's needs that they are in the best position to help prioritize the features that deliver the largest amount of revenue in a recurring payment business: existing customers.

Marketing

Just as CSMs know what features customers require to derive more value from the product, they also have deep insight into what features are currently driving the most value. This information needs to be conveyed regularly to the Marketing team, which can use the information to sharpen its messaging around benefits. Also, CSMs are the first in the company who can identify potential success stories to form the basis of referrals and content marketing opportunities. This insight should be conveyed in a formal process, either via a periodic update or meeting.

The best way to acquire the right customers is to tailor your pitches appropriately. The knowledge that the Customer Success team should have about what makes the best customers needs to be applied as early as you can in the process. In the best case, the Customer Success executive should even have veto authority over marketing campaigns.

There is also a significant overlap between the Customer Success Education role and the production of educational content by the marketing team. In an ideal situation a single resource can produce the content necessary to educate both the market and existing customers, but it is often the case that the content required varies by target.

Special Topic: The Need for Customer Marketing

You may or may not have noticed, but many of the activities I outlined in "Doing the Work" and subsequent chapters on the various stages of Customer Success involved tasks that would traditionally be reserved for the Marketing function.

For instance, when a new product feature is released, who should send the notification to existing customers? After all, I have talked in this book about how all communication with existing customers should include the customer's specific context and provide insight – in a word, such communication should be intimate.

I am reminded of a recent email campaign we sent at Totango. The campaign was exactly this, a new feature announcement, but the open rate was north of 65%. That is unheard of in the world of email, and on researching it I found that we had targeted only users who were already functional on the rest of the feature set and who had high Health Indicators. The email had made reference to their specific usage data in the subject line.

This level of intimacy should be the standard in communicating with customers, which leads me to believe that we should have a new marketing function specific to existing customers. This Customer Marketing function should be a matrixed group with reporting lines into the Chief Marketing Officer as well as the Chief Customer Officer.

Chapter 11:

Farming Tools

Think back on the changed world I described earlier in the book, a world of recurring revenue business, digitization, and increased customer expectations. If there is one thing these all have in common it is an increased flow of information and an increased need to react to information quickly and efficiently. The tools you use for your Customer Success machine will directly affect whether you are able to do that. Fortunately new tools are available that address the key needs of synthesizing, analyzing, and acting on data.

The Limitations of CRM

Many businesses, particularly SaaS businesses, use Customer Relationship Management (CRM) tools such as Salesforce, SugarCRM, Microsoft Dynamics or Zoho as the hub for their customer management. There are real limitations to these platforms, however.

First, they are designed to solve an account management problem rather than a data problem. What this means is that they are basically a static repository for information about the account, rather than dynamic reflections on the actual use of your product at the user level. Another way to put this is that CRM solutions are linear in their view: they are designed to help sales-people manage a funnel of opportunities down to a "closed-won" stage and are focused on a single success metric: to maximize revenue from opportunities. But managing customers is an iterative process with multi-ple vectors pulling and pushing towards a multitude of success metrics, some of which are commercial, others of which aren't.

Second, while many of them have modules, they are not truly designed to combine and interpret the data signals from any source that might reflect information about your customers, from social networks to your internal database to publicly available information.

Third, and importantly, CRM systems are not designed to trigger workflows based on customer actions. They can generate reports, but they do not prioritize CSM actions based on customer related metrics.

THE RISE OF CUSTOMER SUCCESS TOOLS

The shortcomings of CRM systems form the backbone for a new class of Customer Success tools. These tools, from companies like Totango, Guidespark, and others, provide Customer Success leaders with the data aggre-gation, signalization, and workflow-triggering capabili-ties that CRM systems lack.

This is an area that is of real interest to me. While this book is intended to give you the why's and how's of Customer Success, I have spent much of my career building software that incorporates the best elements of farming your customers into a single platform that allows you to proactively influence customer lifetime value.

You can think of the instructions in this book as the "manual" version of customer success – one that lets you create Excel versions of a Customer Success Scorecard, for instance. I strongly believe that if you take the lessons of this book and apply them even to a limited degree, you will significantly improve your business. But doing so using Excel and makeshift tools will be inefficient and in some cases ineffective.

The fact is that the "manual" version of what I describe is very, very complex. The reality of hundreds of customers and dozens of metrics requires software to manage. Quite simply, it is the difference between manual farming and automated farming, and most business leaders understand the benefits of the latter.

Aggregation

Today's Customer Success tools are able to pull in data from any source that is pertinent to understanding your customer. This might include any or all of the following:

- Usage, utilization, KPIs, user and customer signals from the service

- Customer feedback and touchpoints

- Sales and marketing systems
- Subscription billing and accounting systems
- Social Networks

Signalization

It is one thing to connect to all those data sources. It is another to be able to combine that information dynamically in ways that filter signal from noise. This is what I term "signalization," the ability of a tool to distill important insights from the ever-increasing mass of customer data being fed into business systems.

Workflow

Given the number of accounts and users overseen by the average CSM, a report is not sufficient. A well-configured dashboard is no longer enough. Even signalized insights are not sufficient to be useful in a fast-paced business environment. Rather, a cutting edge Customer Success tool needs to be able to translate those insights into prioritized action items for CSMs to carry out. Moreover, it needs to provide sufficient contextual data so that the CSM can fix the problem in the personalized, relevant way I have discussed earlier in the book.

Also, a well-functioning Customer Success organization doesn't just do Success Plays and then reallocate resources to other activities. Instead, Success Plays are cumulative...the ones that do, in fact, affect driver metrics need to remain in the company's workflow and must scale far more slowly than your Customer Success team. A good technology solution allows you to do this, building up the volume of concurrent Success Plays you run while also increasing your customer base without a proportional increase in your Customer Success team.

Chapter 12

Conclusion

I've written this book as a reference for business leaders who are building, growing and optimizing their customer success strategy, teams, and execution engines.

As the co-founder and CEO of Totango, I've been fortunate to take part in the birth and growth of the Customer Success industry, which is still in its infancy. But I've seen enough to know that Customer Success is something that will only grow in importance and which most business leaders haven't fully grasped yet.

I wanted to do two things with this book: share my high level thoughts on this new paradigm, and, and at the same time, to provide a practical guide to understand, design, implement and most importantly, iterate Customer Success execution models.

But if you are only going to remember one thing from this book, remember to farm - don't hunt.

CHAPTER 13

Special Topics

TOPIC 1: CUSTOMER SUCCESS AND THE COMPANY LIFECYCLE

By: Boaz Maor

Rome was not built in one day. Neither will your grove be planted in one. Most farmers start with a small grove of a few trees, learn which ones hold, which ones die, which ones need more or less water, more or less fertilizer, more or less sun, more or less assistance and so on. Over time, they perfect their formulas and processes to help their grove grow and then, capitalizing on their early success, they expand their grove. They might add more trees, add more varieties of trees, expand to other territories and so on.

Just like the grove, companies also grow through stages. Most start-ups go through relatively "standard" phases referred to in the industry as: Inception, Build, Growth, Expansion, and Maturity.

Each stage has a number of characteristics that define it, namely:

Phase:	Inception	Build	Growth	Expansion
Product Maturity:	Alpha	Beta	GA	Multiproduct
Process Maturity:	None	Repetitive	Standards	Insights
Customer Types:	Innovators	Innovators	Early Adop.	Early Major.
# of Customers:	Few	Dozens	Hundreds	Thousands

A farmer establishing her own farm is likely to do most of the work on her own, partially to save money (since there is no income yet from the young trees) and partially due to personal investment (since she is so invested in her grove, she wants to and can get involved with every tree). The first few hires she will bring in are likely people who can either help with very critical work-streams or people who can wear multiple hats and engage in lots of different activities as needed. As the grove grows, the need for work grows, but also the need for more specialized knowledge.

Let's use watering as an example. If, early on, the farmer waters her tiny grove on her own using a hose, when it grows she will at some point need someone who can do that job so she can do other jobs. Over time, as the grove grows, manual labor might not be cost-effective anymore and an automated watering system is needed, maybe even one that can fertilize at the same time. When the groves grows even more and the farmer becomes more sophisticated, she might look for experts in watering technologies that can adjust to the specific needs of each tree using sensors deployed next to each one, sending continuous data to a mission control system. The skillset of the person in charge of watering has changed from a physically strong person (hopefully with some experience watering groves) to a Water System Engineer with an advanced degree in Computer Science, depth of knowledge in big data analytics with specific experience in the special type of trees you are growing and hopefully some experience in IOT (Internet of Things)...

As they grow, companies too must adjust their structure and realign their teams to the new reality of their larger and more sophisticated organization, serving larger volumes of more sophisticated and demanding customers. When your company is very small, in its Inception and sometimes even during the Build phase, you are not likely to have a dedicated Customer Success person on-board. Quite frankly, everybody in the company is probably involved with every customer: if your CEO is a technical person, she is probably the person deploying the solution with the help of every person on the product team. If she is a business person, she probably acts as the sales and relationship management person, while your head of engineering provides professional services and technical support.

At some point, however, you need someone dedicated to this function. As noted earlier in this book, your first hire into what will at some point be the Customer Success organization is a CSM: the person responsible for maximizing the value the customers can gain from your solutions. The characteristics of this person depend on your product and the market, but the first few people are likely to be fairly technical with strong customer relationship and project management skills. This person will have to manage a small set of customers, serving them with a very immature product, following a process that barely exists, while everybody in the company claims that "we can't fail with this strategic customer." Over time, of course, you will hire more people into this role.

But, what separates a good Customer Service team from a great one is the ability to time appropriately not only when to hire additional people, but also how to change the job description and characteristics of the people you hire.

The dimensions impacting your team's structure the most, and the ones you must most carefully consider include:

1. The maturity of the market: the less mature the market (read: the more unique your product category is), the more evangelizers you need, as opposed to the next point:

2. The maturity of your product: the less mature the product, the more hand-holding the customer needs.

3. The maturity of your deployment process: the easier it is for the customer to get on-boarded and become self-sufficient, the more streamlined your organization can be (fewer roles, less complexity and fewer people touching the customer).

4. The size of your customer base: the more customers you have to manage, the more important it is

to move quickly towards automating activities in order to control costs.

5. The extent of the Land-and-Expand strategy: the more potential for expansion there is with your customers, the more involved you want to be with them over time and the more quickly you would want to move commercial responsibilities over from Sales to the Customer Success organization.

All of the above dimensions change over time. As they change, you must change your organization structure to match the changing needs. It is important for the head of the Customer Success team to identify as early as possible in their role (and check every few months) where they are in each of those dimensions and how well their organization matches them. Then, they should establish a plan that is at least one step ahead of where they are today so they have a clear line of sight towards the future needs of the organization when they establish the team's structure, key roles, job descriptions, and characteristics of successful candidates.

Key roles to focus on in each phase:

1. **Inception:** In most start-ups, there will not be a dedicated Customer Success person during Inception phase.

2. **Build:** This is normally when the first CSM is hired. A relatively technical person with good project management and customer relationship management skills. In many cases this person will come from either a professional services background

or an engineering one. In some cases, you should also hire a Technical Support person during this phase, although this function might be covered by the Engineering team.

3. **Growth:** this is when most Customer Success teams are formed and developed. Normally a head for the team (at either a VP or Director level) is hired here and a preliminary structure is defined with key roles or small sub-teams being:

▶ CSM (on-boarding and on-going management of the customer deployment).

▶ Tech Support (time-based management of the technical relations with the customer day-to-day users).

▶ Professional Services (project based work to develop and/or configure the solution to the needs of the customer).

▶ Training (getting knowledge to customers) and Customer Relationship Management (managing commercial relations).

This is a critical phase, as this is when the foundations of process (deployment methodology, management reporting, customer dashboards, customer communications, etc.) are built. For many companies, this is when teams from different organizations (Tech Support from Engineering, Account Management from Sales, Training form Marketing, etc.) are combined into a single Customer Success team.

And this is when you might want to consider altering the characteristics of your hires <u>from generalists to specialists.</u>

4. **Expansion:** The main difference during the Expansion phase is the speed at which new customers are added. If you've done a good job building a solid foundation during the Growth phase, in this stage you can scale by adding more people into the established structures. The reality is that you are likely to need to continue to divide the teams and roles here into more specific ones in order to enable the development of centers of excellence (COE) in specific areas. Some of the key areas can be customer industry, your product lines, customer stages (trial, on-boarding, training, on-going) and more.

The characteristics of successful candidates into the roles you have should be fine-tuned to reflect the knowledge and expertise you wish to generate. Also, this is when your CEO is likely to start pressing you to curtail costs as the organization grows quickly. This is when a strong Customer Operations team is critical to enable the automation of activities such as reporting, customer communications and marketing, transactional commercial work and more.

TOPIC 2: MANAGING COSTS

Customer Acquisition Costs

You would think that the amount of money it takes to acquire a customer, also known as the Customer Acquisition Cost or CAC, would be of little concern to the Customer Success organization. While this is generally true, it is worth pointing out an important fact:

The cost of upselling an existing customer is a fraction of the cost of acquiring a new customer.

The way the SaaS industry measures CAC is as a ratio – how much does it cost to buy a dollar of annual revenue by acquiring a new customer? The median in 2015 was $1.18.* The same measure can be applied to the cost of acquiring an incremental dollar from an existing customer in an upsell. That figure? $0.28. And for renewing an existing customer? $0.11. It is worth noting that many organizations do not book the costs of their CSMs against the CAC.

CAC is a tricky metric, because most companies do a rough guesstimate once, and then assume it to be an absolute ever after. Obviously it changes, and you should seek to update it to reflect changes in your cost and revenue structure.

The Relative Costs of Acquiring a Subscription Dollar in 2015

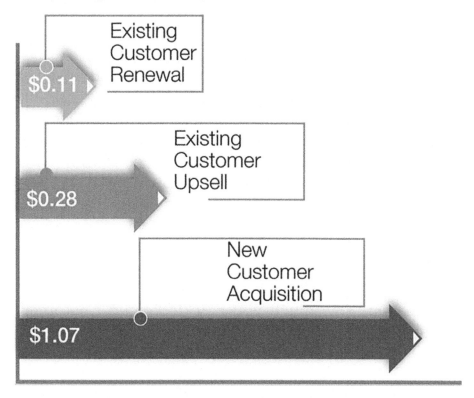

It's very clear that the most efficient way to "buy" a dollar of new revenue is to get it from an existing customer, and the Customer Success Machine is what allows you to do this.

Those figures are "fully loaded," meaning that they take into account all of the costs required to achieve that sale, renewal, or upsell, including the cost of the Customer Success team. As the leader of that team, however, you want to focus on the portion of those costs that are directly attributable to you.

*2015 Pacific Crest Securities Report on the State of SaaS.

Customer Retention Costs

The costs that the firm incurs to renew and upsell a customer are known as Customer Retention Costs or CRC. While the above data on the relative efficiency of renewing and upselling versus acquiring a new customer is compelling, it is all too easy to have CRC run away from you unless you track it closely. But CRC really requires emphasizing and should be the foundation for the CS budget process.

The components of CRC include:

Salaries: how much you pay dedicated Customer Success employees, including Technical, Support, Training, Commercial, and any other resources.

Content Production: internal or outsourced production costs for slide decks, webinars, infographics, and any other content that needs to be produced to support the customer.

Training Events: venues, meals, and any other physical costs for training the customer.

Until you have factored all of these costs against the benefit of keeping and growing your customers then you have not properly accounted for the economics of your business.

TOPIC 3: TECHNOLOGY AND THE DIFFERENCE BETWEEN MANAGING ACCOUNTS VS. MANAGING USERS

Technology has enabled us to view customer activity at a very granular level. So when I talk in the book about managing customers through their lifecycle and running Success Plays to influence their Driver Metrics I refer not only to overall accounts, but also to individual users. This distinction is important to keep in mind, because accounts are not monolithic.

After all, individual users can each be at different stages of development. It gets extremely complicated, of course, but people come and go from companies all the time – so all of a sudden the tree in your grove that you think looks healthy is actually only 'half' healthy.

Or, the CSM can have a great relationship with the product champion, but other users within the organization may not have the same commitment.

Generally speaking, the same lessons that I have laid out here at the account level can be applied at the individual user or user group lesson through the use of technology.

TOPIC 4: THE CUSTOMER SUCCESS MANIFESTO

I have found that one of the hardest things in evolving organizations to a Customer Success orientation is in getting people to think differently. Farming is part of this, obviously, in that it is a new high-level view of the customer. More tactically, though, I have found it useful to encourage teams to think about very specific concepts to prioritize. I have summarized these in what I call the Customer Success Manifesto, which I outline below and can be found at http://www.thecustomersuccessmanifesto.com :

Principles of the Customer Success Manifesto

1 **Value**
—— Over——
customer management

2 **Customer Actions**
—— Over——
words

3 **Real-time sensors**
—— Over——
historical snapshots

4 **Contextual Engagement**
—— Over——
periodic check-ins

5 **All Customers**
—— Over——
over high value customers

6 **All Users**
—— Over——
buyers and decision makers

TOPIC 5: A PLAN FOR A NEW CUSTOMER SUCCESS VP

By: Omer Gottlieb

Congratulations! You've been selected to start or revamp a Customer Success program at your company. So where do you begin? It's important to start off on the right foot. Here are the steps you should take in the first 90 days to fully understand your role, your team, and your business.

FIRST 30 DAYS: SET A BASELINE

Your first job is to understand what you're walking into. This is the time to find any problem areas and establish where the team stands at the moment. To do this you must understand the status of your customer base and as well as the health of these accounts.

Step 1: Get visibility into your customer base

Understand what data is available and what reports can be generated to provide you with good insight into your customer base. Some of this basic information might include:

- Customer count: how is it measured and how is it reported.

- On-boarding process: scope, duration, effort, customer feedback.

- On-going usage: what adoption statistics can you report on and capture from customers.
- Customers by segment
  - ▶ Industries
  - ▶ Products
  - ▶ Size of company
  - ▶ Size of engagement (MRR)
  - ▶ Geography

...and other parameters that will enable you to get a perspective on your customers.

Build a renewal map: Given that there is immediate revenue impact, renewals are important area to focus on. What is the status of these accounts, is there an immediate problem you have to solve or is this a future concern that you can deal with down the road? Understanding where these customers stand will help you establish your immediate priorities.

Identify problem areas: As you start reviewing where you are today, you will quickly see problem areas that need to be addressed. These could be issues related to onboarding, training, support, the product, your engagement model and process – anything. Highlighting these early will help you build a plan to move forward.

Step 2: Learn more about your customers

Analyze churned and happy customers: Take a look at the customers who've churned and renewed in the last 6-12 months to see what the data tells you about these groups. Are there key milestones or events that are indicators of positive or negative performance? Collecting these data points will help you hone in on what indicators your team should be using so they can proactively manage their customer accounts.

Identify your champions: These users can be relied on to provide you with anecdotal feedback and additional insights to how these accounts are using your product. It's important to introduce yourself to their contacts because they'll provide accurate and honest feedback that can be leveraged by your and your team.

Meet your customers: Start taking time to meet with your customers, closed lost opportunities and even accounts that have just churned. As the "new guy" you can ask more questions and get greater insights into what happened in these accounts. These don't need to be sales meetings but instead fact-finding missions for you to get a better understanding of what you do well and what you need to do better.

Step 3: Learn more about your team

Analyze your team: The first 30 days is your opportunity to get to know your team and establish their strengths and weaknesses. What are the gaps that you need to address? There are lots of different ways to organize your team based on the complexity of the product, the roles and responsibilities, and the pay structure.

Analyze the processes that are in place: Understanding how your organization gets things done is something you need to understand at a very granular level. This includes but is not limited to:

- What steps are taken?
- Who is doing what?
- What works and where are the challenges?
- Where does the organization stall?
- Which features are easiest to deploy and which are hardest?
- Which features have the best feedback from customers and which the worst?

...and more. The point is that your understanding of these processes should be detailed so that you can start to improve on them.

FIRST 60 DAYS: Define an Action Plan

Once you've taken stock of what the current situation is, it's time to work on your action plan. Based on what you learned, what are areas that can be fixed quickly and make a big impact vs. major gaps that will require more time to solve.

Step 1: Define your customer cycle

Determine the right customer segmentation: You may already have segmentation in place; now is the time to determine if this is done correctly. Segmentation will help you determine not only how your team interacts with customers but also how you evaluate their use of the product.

Map your Customer Cycle: Taking the milestones and events that you learned, now you can spend time defining the customer journey for each segment you identify. What path should the customer take that leads them to value and in turn renewal and expansion? What are the actions that lead toward churn along the way?

Step 2: Implement an early warning system

Once you have the data and the customer journey mapped you can set up alerts for your customer base that allow you to address problems immediately as opposed to waiting for time based check-ins. *An early warning system* enables your team to focus on the accounts that need help or have the most opportunities as opposed to only managing those with the largest account value.

Step 3: Create executive dashboards

Establishing clear ways of measuring and communicating success is imperative to driving support for your team. In order to make the conversation very easy, you want to build executive dashboards that highlight your key metrics and indicate the progress that you've been making. Key metrics will vary based on your organization but may include: number/portion of customers in each state (on-boarding, maturing, expanding), overall customer health, % churn, *Customer Retention Cost (CRC)*, portfolio score, engagement.

Step 4: Design your engagement model

As you build the internal processes to identify and measure your customer base, you'll want to establish how your Customer Success Managers engage with their customers. For accounts having trouble with onboarding, what tools should be leveraged to get them on track? For customers with renewal coming up, are there specific meetings that can be used to ensure the customers are on track?

Figuring out the best course of action should still be left to the determination of the CSM but here are some engagement models you can consider.

- **Quarterly Business Review:** A scheduled review with the account. This is great for high touch customers who may have custom configurations.

- **Surveys:** Can be run periodically or based on a customer action, such as at the end of the on-boarding phase, as an impassive way to collect feedback.

- **Meetings:** This is a good way for your team to understand what is going on in an account as well as build relationships with the key stakeholders.

- **Advisory Board:** Designed to provide feedback from key accounts that can help you make executive roadmap decisions.

- **Training:** Can be used for onboarding, with the release of new features or even for new users added to the account.

- **Webinars:** One to many presentations that can help your customers continue to move along their journey.

Step 5: Build the right team for the future

At this point you should define the future state of the organization, the one that will be successful in 3-6 months. This will allow you to define the charter and mission with the team.

Then you can begin filling in the gaps that were identified early on: this may be simply hiring new Customer Success Managers or adding Customer Success Engineers that can focus on the more technical aspects of the product. There may be training required for your current customer base that will help them improve their position. This is also the time to make sure you have correctly distributed your customer base to each member of your team.

FIRST 90 DAYS: BUILD SMART, REPEATABLE, SCALABLE PROGRAMS

Now that you have identified that areas of improvement and defined your action plan, it's time to create programs that can be used by your team. These will help you quickly expand and optimize the process by which you engage with your customers and allow your team to become even more proactive.

Note: Accomplishing everything I lay out here is a very aggressive goal. The 90-day guideline is just that, a guideline.

Step 1: Roll out Customer Success programs

Drive more value and improve customer experience with clearly defined programs that keep customers on their journey to success. These programs should identify and mitigate any potential churn risks in the customer base, but they also need to highlight potential growth opportunities.

Step 2: Make assumptions, measure and analyze

Once you've identified the key areas of focus to improve your Customer Success team, it's important to make sure you have a continuous feedback loop in place. As you move forward in your plan you need to continue to collect, analyze, and refine how your team engages with their customers.

Appendix 1:

Common Questions

I get all kinds of questions about Customer Success that don't fit neatly into the flow of the book. I include some of the more common ones here.

What should be the ratio between a CSM and number of accounts managed?

As every CSM owns a portfolio, you would want to scale your customer success organization based on value. As an example, every CSM should own a portfolio initially valued at $2M. If the specific CSM is dealing with low value accounts worth on average $2K each, it means that they have 1000 accounts in their portfolio, and, on the other hand, if they deal with average ACV of $200K, it means that they have 10 accounts in their portfolio. For obvious reasons managing 1000 accounts will require relying mainly on automation, while managing 10 accounts could allow high-touch model to manage a portfolio.

How should I prioritize my team's work—which accounts they should be working on?

If you have a bit of time, I suggest you read Chapter 5, "Doing The Work." The main message in that chapter regarding customer prioritization is that you should focus on the Success Plays that have the greatest impact on value over time. To identify these Success Plays you need to have set up a Customer Success Scorecard that divides your customers into distributions based on a variety of indicators. You can do this manually, but across a large customer set you will need technology to surface the customers that are in high-risk/high-potential segments and work on those first.

How do I know if my team is productive and effective?

If you have taken the time to create an effective Customer Success Scorecard, the distributions of customers into high and low value segments will be an important indicator of your team and individual outcomes. However, you should also set up systems to track knowhow indicators (via testing), activity indicators (via volume measures such as number of calls) and implementation indicators (measuring the number and type of Success Plays the team and individual uses). Combined, these measurements of know-how, activity, implementation, and outcomes will give you a sense of how well your team is doing.

I have a retention problem—what do I do?

When you have a churn problem you first need to understand it. Bucket the reasons why customers churn into categories and asses the biggest impact. Churn categories could fall into:

- They never really implemented your product

- Onboarding project was slow and incomplete

- Customer experienced many service disruptions (quality)

- There was a mismatch between customer's initial expectation and needs and what was delivered

- The project got cancelled, priorities have shifted, champion left

- Company went out of business

- The customer found a different solution and switched over

Based on the key reasons, implement the programs that impact those reasons by changing the right drivers.

What are the main KPIs I should be measuring and improving?

There is no way to cover all the metrics discussed in this book, and all of them "triangulate" to help you achieve your results. Briefly, however, the most valuable outcome measures are Renewal, Upsell, Churn, and Cost.

Should I have my CS team be responsible for upsells?

Yes, however the best practice developing in the industry is that the upsell transaction should be a different individual from the lead CSM on an account in order to maintain the CSM's trusted advisor role.

What should I include in an Account Review?

At minimum you should be showing your customer the following:

- A review of their ROI metrics, which is the best way of demonstrating value.

- A review of their per user usage patterns, with a view to showing the breadth of your impact.

- A review of their capacity utilization so that they are naturally aware of upsell and cross-sell opportunities without you having to push them.

- A review of their business results that are the outcome of using your product.

- A review of the feature set they are using, with suggestions of further features that could be used to increase value.

What are the main processes I should be running?

If you think of processes as what I have termed Success Plays in the book, you should be making sure that you are running Success Plays that onboard and nurture your accounts as effectively as possible. For more details on what Success Plays to run in each phase please see the relevant chapters in the book.

What should I report to my board?

Board reporting needs to be a balance of outcome metrics, which include the four I mention in the book (note that these are specific to Customer Success – I assume revenue is covered elsewhere):

1. Renewals

2. Upsell and Cross-Sell

3. Churn

4. Costs

...and of leading indicators of driver measures:

1. Adoption

2. Usage

3. Operational

4. Customer satisfaction/relationship

Appendix 2:

Glossary

ACRC   Annual Customer Retention Cost

ACV   Annual Contract Value

AE   Account Executive

AM   Account Manager

ARR   Annual Recurring Revenue

B2B   Business to Business

B2C   Business to Consumer

BDR   Business Development Representative

CAC   Client Acquisition Cost, the amount to acquire a single client

CCO   Chief Customer Officer

CEO   Chief Executive Officer

CLV   Customer Lifetime Value

CR   Conversion Ratio

CRC	Client Retention Cost, the cost to retain a client for 12 months
CRM	Customer Relationship Management (platform)
CRO	Chief Revenue Officer
CSM	Customer Success Manager
CSM	Customer Success Manager
FAE	Field Account Executive
LIVE	Client who has been onboarded and using the solution
MAS	Marketing Automation Software (platform)
MRR	Monthly Recurring Revenue
PM	Product Manager
RoI	Return on Investment
SaaS	Software as a Service
SDR	Sales Development Representative

Final Notes

For more information on Customer Success I recommend you read the Totango Blog at:

http://www.totango.com/blog/

Also, I host a yearly conference with Customer Success industry leaders in which we cover the material in this book in even greater depth. More information can be found here:

http://customersuccesssummit.com/

Last, there are several active Linkedin groups on the topic of Customer Success:

Customer Success Executives: **http://www.linkedin.com/groups/4668172/profile**

The Customer Success Forum: **http://www.linkedin.com/groups/1913401/profile**

Customer Success: **http://www.linkedin.com/groups/1805358/profile**

About the Author

Guy Nirpaz is the founder and CEO of Totango, a Silicon Valley based firm whose product enables Customer  Success. Guy loves people and technology and has dedicated his career to improving the way in which people do business. Prior to starting Totango he was EVP of Engineering at GigaSpaces and Chief Architect at Mercury, two significant players in big data and software.

Fun Facts: Guy moonlights as the lead guitarist in a rock band based out of his garage in Palo Alto and used to command a tank battalion ... as well as having grown oranges.

Made in the USA
Coppell, TX
15 June 2021